You Wouldn't Hike Without a Compass!

Don't Buy Health Insurance Without This Book

Simplifying and Explaining Health Vocabulary

D.L. Byrd

Preface

Why this book? I'm a life and health insurance agent licensed in various states throughout the country. I've also worked on concierge service teams helping people figure out their claims, verifying prescriptions covered, determining if pre-authorizations are approved, and explaining how plans work.

I found the best way to educate policyholders was to explain health terminology using a "it's like…" method. This method usually opened the eyes of policyholders and gave them power to make better decisions.

Someone once said, "Knowledge is Power!" So, in an effort to help people understand insurance terms, I've put together this book using the same "it's like" method to simplify the terms.

You Wouldn't Hike Without a Compass...

I hope through these short chapters the reader will receive knowledge and power to make better healthcare decisions. In the short term, this knowledge can help save money by preventing unnecessary expenses. In this case, the little guy (or future policyholder) can win!

Dedication

This book is dedicated to Nathan, Alicia, and baby Isabella Martin. What your local hospital tried to do is horrible! I'm thrilled we were able to exponentially reduce your hospital bill from four figures to two digits, saving your future tax return.

Your unfortunate (almost disastrous) experience has prompted me to write this book in hopes of helping others! So, enjoy and consider the first copy yours! God bless, and love you!

Introduction – Like the Wizard of Oz

Selecting a healthcare plan is like fearfully visiting the "Great and Powerful Oz" only to discover "Oz" is a feeble old man hiding and blowing smoke from behind a curtain. Once the truth has emerged, all fear is wiped away and the feeble old guy becomes a resource to solve the problems of the scarecrow, tin man, and lion.

The purpose of this book is to provide simple definitions to help you shop for healthcare plans. Knowledge truly is powerful!

For example, monthly premiums can be simply defined as monthly costs you pay the insurance company; annual deductibles (in most cases) are annual contributions made before the health insurance company will spend a penny toward claims (or medical bills)!

So, what becomes of your annual contributions? They are used to pay medical bills of others! What? That's like having an excellent driving record but being forced to pay for a bad driver's accident. Seems silly and unfair, right? That's why it's necessary to understand health insurance terms to make better decisions when purchasing a plan.

Once you've been provided with cross references, you'll be able to select plans that fit the needs of you and your family, saving you money in the process. Before we start pulling back the curtain, let me raise another curtain.

Acknowledgements   – Raising the Curtain

First, a huge thank you to my best friend Brenda K. Davis. You are not only like a sister; you are a sister! You have been a total encouragement and a blessing. All the years you spent teaching kindergarten—simplifying reading, writing, and math to 5-year-olds— rubbed off. I now know the power of keeping things simple and building on concepts. Also, thanks for always being an encouraging cheerleader; no wonder you're a "Rodel Award" teacher"! You're awesome!

Next, thanks to my crazy friend, Steven S. Weis. You have the overwhelming talent of keeping me laughing. Your humor (as sick as it can be at times) has kept me focused on the goal of helping others understand insurance terms! Also, thanks for reminding me of terms I'd forgotten and keeping me on track. Never change, you're a good crazy!

Now let's turn our attention to the other curtain that needs to be ripped down instead of raised. The curtain that cloaks and causes fear when dealing with health insurance terms.

Contents

You Wouldn't Hike Without a Compass...

Chapter 1 – The Players

In football, each position has a title and purpose. The quarterback receives the football and passes to a wide receiver. The offensive linemen protects the quarterback from getting taken down by the opposing team's offense.

Once you know the title and purpose of each player, you can begin to enjoy the game and its strategies.

Same with health insurance. Once you understand the terminology and descriptions, you can effectively find plans better tailored for you and your family and save money.

Let's start with four simple terms common to health insurance statements:

You Wouldn't Hike Without a Compass...

The *Provider* - simply those who "provide" a service (i.e., doctors, nurses, specialists, pharmacists, urgent care facilities, and hospitals).

The *insured* or *policyholder* - that's you! You are the one who's "insured". You are also the one who "holds the policy".

Insurance company or *Insurer* - they of course provide the policy or coverage.

Policy - technically a contract between you and the insurance company. *You* have the most power over the policy. The insurance company can only void the policy if you stop paying monthly payments or inform the insurance company you want to cancel the plan. You can terminate the policy whenever you want (however, it's recommended you don't cancel or terminate unless you already have another policy in place).

Just a quick point, most health costs center around the following:

1) age

2) gender

3) household income

4) state and county

5) zip code

6) height and weight

7) pre-existing illnesses

The following chapters explain terminology and information helpful to purchase the right plan for you and your family. There are behind-the-scenes companies that play a role in the cost of your coverage. We'll try to cover that information in this book. For the first read, consider following the chapters in chronological order.

Chapter 2 – MIB (Medical Information Bureau)

How are previous health issues discovered by insurance companies? Information is discovered through the MIB—no, not "Men in Black", but by the Medical Information Bureau, also known as MIB.

Think of MIB like the credit bureau. The MIB has been around since the early 1900s and is owned by insurance companies. MIB was created to protect insurance companies against fraud.

Remember, "Honesty is always the best policy." You can contact the MIB and request a copy of your record. As of this writing, there are no charges or fees to get a copy. At least one free copy can be provided each year. To request a copy of your MIB, contact MIB at MIB.com.

If anything is incorrect on the MIB, MIB is very good about investigating and correcting its records. Give them a call or contact them online.

MIB does not collect doctor's statements or reports, nor underwriting files resulting from insurance denials. MIB has records of prescription history, driving records, and information related to hazardous hobbies (e.g. bull riding, hot air balloon riding, bungee cord jumping, etc.).

If looking for coverage through private insurance companies, MIB is a great resource to help refresh your memory of former health conditions.

MIB information can also be a resource for other types of insurances such as life insurance. MIB also offers information to other organizations such as unclaimed life property, etc.

Again, start your research with the MIB by going to MIB.com.

Chapter 3 – Monthly Premiums

Now let's look at the insurance term, *premium*. What is a premium? Let's grab our decoder ring.

Think of health insurance premiums as simply monthly payments. After all, monthly car premiums are typically called car *payments*. Monthly mortgages are simply house payments. Monthly health insurance premiums, well, they're really only monthly health insurance payments. So, why not call them what they are and clear the nebulous air?

Eliminating the deciphering process can be a major step in shifting the power into your hands. Premiums…just the cost paid each month (by you, the policyholder) to have health insurance coverage. Again, simply put, monthly payments (the monthly costs) are what you pay to keep your health plan active. If you don't pay your monthly payments, you will end up with no insurance! Simple.

When shopping health insurance premiums, it's important that apple-to-apple coverages are considered. For example, are you covered for lab work, primary care visits, urgent and emergency visits, and telemedicine? When dealing with government plans, are you comparing bronze plans to bronze plans instead of bronze to silver?

A common question is, "Are monthly premiums applied to anything such as 'Maximum Out of Pocket' (explained in a later chapter)?" The answer is no. Monthly payments are not added to maximum out of pocket.

As with anything else, shop around during open enrollment (OE) for best coverage and pricing for yourself or you and your family. The back of this book provides an area to jot down prices, coverages, etc. to compare the apples-to-apples comparison.

Chapter 4 – Annual Deductibles

Now what about *deductibles*? What can deductibles be compared to in layman's terms? Let's start with an example.

"Before ABC Health Insurance Company (a fictitious company), helps pay your health bills, you must first pay an annual donation!"

"WHAT?"

Well, health insurance companies don't call it a donation, they call the collection "Annual Deductibles". Simply put, annual deductibles are like giving forced donations.

Until the deductible is reached, the insurance company will pay very little or nothing at all toward your medical bills. So when shopping health insurance plans, think of deductibles as the other "d" word—donations on top of your monthly payments!

You may ask, "Are monthly insurance payments (premiums) put toward fulfilling annual donations (deductibles)?"

Nope!

"No? Then what counts toward annual deductibles (donations) to decrease the set amount?"

Glad you asked! Let's start with the shorter list of "what is not applied to annual deductibles".

Again, monthly insurance payments (premiums) are not applied to the annual deductible. Here's an example:

If your monthly premium is $200 and your annual deductible is $3,000, the $200 monthly premium will not be applied to nor lower your annual deductible.

"What about copays to doctors, urgent cares, or hospitals?"

Another resounding "no". Copays and coinsurance (both terms we'll decipher in the following chapters) typically are not applied to the annual deductible.

"So, if premiums, copays, and coinsurance are not applied to annual deductibles, what is?" Good question!

Out of pocket costs beyond monthly premiums, copays, and coinsurances are applied toward annual deductibles.

Consider the following scenario:

You have a $3,000 annual deductible. After paying your primary care doctor's $30 copay, the doctor decides to order an x-ray. The x-ray's cost is $200. The insurance company receives the $200 claim (or bill) and negotiates the claim down to $75.

If you have not met your annual deductible, you will be billed the $75.

The $75 billed to you will be subtracted from your $3,000 deductible, reducing your annual deductible to $2,925.

If you have a high deductible and seldom require medical attention, you'll probably never reach your annual deductible (or see it reach $0)! Therefore, you'll continue donating money to the health insurance company while paying monthly premiums and copays.

D.L. Byrd

On the other hand, if you frequently have procedures done, you'll probably reach your annual deductible. Once your annual deductible is met, the insurance company will begin to contribute to the cost of your care.

Consequently, unhealthy policyholders experience more benefits from standard health insurance compared to healthy policyholders because healthy insured seldom meet their annual deductible. Healthy insured may want to consider checking costs with private insurance plans that do not require annual deductibles and copays.

Make sure when shopping for health insurance plans to verify what the annual deductible (or donation) will be; what monthly premiums (monthly payments) will be; what copays are for primary care doctors, specialists, urgent care visits; or hospital visits will cost. Consider adjusting the plan based on what you need and will use.

As you've discovered, until the annual deductible (or donation) is met, all you're doing is providing contributions or donations to the insurance company.

You Wouldn't Hike Without a Compass...

Again, shop your next insurance plan based on annual deductibles, annual premium, coverage (i.e., lab work, medical supplies, etc.) and in/out-of-network coverage.

Chapter 5 – Copays

Things have changed over the decades. You used to be able to walk into a saloon and buy your whiskey at the bar! Now, some saloons have a "cover charge" with big guys called bouncers protecting the entrance.

Before you can go into the saloon, you must pay a gal sitting behind a window (usually near the entrance). Once paid, the bouncer lets you into the saloon to purchase drinks from the bar.

Copays! What are they? Like cover-charged nightclubs, they're the cost you pay before you can see the physician. Copays are typically required when visiting doctors' offices, urgent care offices, or hospitals.

Once paid, someone eventually opens a door, calls your name, and escorts you back to the physician—word of caution, don't call the person escorting you a bouncer. You may end up with a black eye in addition to the original cause of the visit.

Again, think of the copay as a cover charge. Of course, you may be asking, why is it called a copay? Words that begin with "co" typically mean two, right?

You're correct, the cost to see the physician is actually more than your copay.

Before a physician or specialist can be part of an insurance plan, the insurance company and the physician agree upon a price a doctor will be paid. The insurance company pays the physician the agreed upon pay (per patient and per visit) and you pay your half to see the doctor (per visit). That's the *co*-pay!

According to Google, cover charge is defined as an "entrance fee" to bars, nightclubs, or fancy restaurants.

If you consider the similar process of seeing a doctor and entering a nightclub, copays and cover charges are very similar.

When looking for health insurance, keep in mind in some cases, once an annual deductible is reached, some or all copays can change to zero dollars per visit. If you have health issues, make sure you ask if the copays will change to zero dollars once the deductible is met.

Also, keep in mind some ACA plans (in certain US states) provide zero annual deductibles and copays based on income and other factors. Make sure you ask questions.

Is a copay the same thing as coinsurance? No. Coinsurance is different (defined and covered in the next chapter). Your copay (unless dropped after the deductible is met) is the same for each visit.

For example, your plan may have a $20 copay to visit the doctor's office, a $40 copay to see a specialist, a $50 copay to visit an urgent care facility, and $100 copay to visit a hospital. Every primary care visit is a $20 cost. Each specialist (i.e., dermatologist; ear, nose, and throat specialist; etc.) will be $40 per visit. It'll be $50 every time you go to urgent care. And any time you go to the hospital, be prepared to pay $100 up front. X-rays, MRIs, leg or arm casts or braces, etc. may be charged an additional out of pocket cost billed to you later. The copay is just to get in the door!

Just a quick recommendation. Unless in extreme emergencies, whenever medical advice is required, consider the following order of contact: 1) Telemedicine (e.g. Call a Nurse, Call a Doctor, etc.); 2) Primary Care Physician; 3) Urgent Care; 4) Hospital. By following this order, you should save yourself a lot of money.

Chapter 6 – Coinsurance

Okay…spin the dial 3 times clockwise and stop on zero…there ya go. Now, turn the dial slowly counterclockwise and stop on 22…good…you're doing fine. Now, turn the dial clockwise and go past zero and stop on 85. Okay, finally turn the dial counterclockwise and stop on 3, then the safe should open.

What? What do you mean there's only $99 and a penny in the safe? We're supposed to split this 50/50.

Okay, I'll tell you what…since you opened the safe with your fingerprints all over the dial, you'll get more. Let's split it $49 for me and $50 and a penny for you, Mugsy. How's that? That's how we'll share it!

Coinsurance...let's talk about coinsurance. *Coinsurance* is a percentage divided between you and the insurance company.

On some policies, once the annual deductible is reached, copays can change to coinsurance, where you only pay a percentage of the cost and the rest is picked up by the insurance company. For example, you (the insured) may pay 20% of the office visit and the insurance company picks up the balance of 80% to pay the complete bill (or claim) to total 100%.

For example, if the office bill is $200, your portion will be $40 (which is 20% of $200) and the insurance company will pay the remaining $160. That's coinsurance.

Let's use a realistic life scenario. You have a policy with the following:

Annual Deductible: $2,500

Coinsurance: 20% (20/80)

Maximum Out of Pocket: $6,000

(Maximum Out of Pocket is covered in the next chapter)

If you were to end up with a serious health issue requiring treatment amounting to $15,000, your plan should work as follows:

First you'd be responsible for the deductible (remember, the deductible always comes first) of $2,500. Subtracting $2,500 from the $15,000 bill leaves an amount due of $12,500. Now that the deductible is out of the way, you are now responsible for the 20% coinsurance. 20% of $12,500 is $2,500. So your total commitment is $5,000 (Deductible + Coinsurance). The insurance company's responsibility is $10,000.

IF the bill had been $20,000 with:

Annual Deductible: $4,000

Coinsurance: 20% (20/80)

Maximum Out of Pocket: $6,000

(Again, Maximum Out of Pocket is covered in the next chapter)

What would your responsibility be? First, you'd have to pay the $4,000 deductible, then you'd be responsible for 20% of the $16,000 balance (i.e., $20,000 minus the $4,000 deductible equals $16,000), which would be $3,200 for a total of $7,200 ($4,000 deductible + $3,200 coinsurance). *However,* since your maximum out of pocket is $6,000, you'd only pay a total of $6,000—the beauty of having a reasonable Maximum Out of Pocket Maximum (MOOP).

Depending on your health situation, a coinsurance scenario can work well or can be a burdensome expense. When shopping for insurance, take into consideration your health situation and see what may work better for you.

Let's take a closer look at MOOP.

Chapter 7 – Maximum Out of Pocket

"Keep pouring, you'll get their attention."

"But no one cares that I'm standing here pouring milk!"

"They'll start caring once the milk overflows."

"And then what?"

"Then you'll have everyone's attention and begin proving your point!"

A lot of things have a maximum limit. In health insurance, there's a *Maximum Out of Pocket* (or MOOP) for each given year. What does that mean? *Once your Maximum Out of Pocket has been reached, the insurance company picks up 100% of covered services for the remainder of the year!*

You Wouldn't Hike Without a Compass...

Understand that MOOP does *not* include monthly premiums nor money spent for services your plan does not cover.

MOOP consist of deductibles, copays, coinsurance, and additional services your plan covers that you've paid before the end of the plan year.

One of the best ways to keep track of payments and determine your MOOP is by keeping copies of the Explanation of Benefits (EOBs, explained in the following chapter). Each time a claim is submitted for a doctor/specialist/urgent care/hospital visit, or when prescriptions or durable medical equipment (DME, explained in a later chapter) are made, an Explanation of Benefits is created by the insurance company. Each EOB should be kept as a reference.

Chapter 8 – Explanation of Benefits

A philatelist collects rare and unique stamps. Numismatists collect rare and unique coins. Rock hounds collect rare or valuable minerals. Someone who has health insurance coverage should collect statements called *Explanation of Benefits*, or EOBs.

After a health insurance plan is started, any claims submitted should trigger an EOB from the insurance company. The EOB is not an item needed in decision-making when purchasing insurance but is very important once the plan is in force, and it deserves mentioning.

An EOB is a statement disclosing the insured's name, date of service (the date the insured was seen), the cost of the service, the amount you owe (and only what you owe and nothing more), reason codes, breakdown of the service, and how much the insurance company will pay for the claim.

When referenced, the EOB can resolve issues related to whether or not an insured owes an office or facility additional money. Here's an example:

A family (due to circumstance) was unable to get help from a primary care physician and could not go to an urgent care facility during regular hours; as a result, they went to a local hospital for help. Their insurance company offered coverage to primary care physicians, urgent care, and hospitals.

Upon attending the hospital, the ER physician confirmed the insured had a serious ear infection and wrote a prescription to resolve the pain. A month later, the hospital sent the insured a $1,200 bill. The EOB indicated the insured only owed $11. The insured contacted the insurance company, explained the hospital was insisting on a full $1,200 payment or the insured would risk having the bill sent to collections. As a result of having the EOB, the insured was able to hand the problem to the insurance company, who resolved the issue.

Again, the EOB is a statement showing the breakdown of services that has taken place. If a service has taken place and you have not received an EOB from the insurance company, it may be the billing department where the services took place may not have submitted a claim.

EOBs also show any denied claims. A good example are health plans that only cover in-network visits (covered in the following chapter) and deny any out-of-network visits. Denied claims are not applied to the Maximum Out of Pocket (MOOP).

Again, adding each EOB's "You Owe" column helps determine if you've reached your Maximum Out of Pocket (MOOP). Once the MOOP is reached, the insurance company picks up cost of services performed for the rest of the year.

Chapter 9 – In-Network versus Out-of-Network

"Yeah, my goofy brother and his friends are up in the treehouse. They said no girls are allowed in their club! We're considered out-of-network, whatever that means!"

Two common terms in health insurance are the terms, *in-network* and *out-of-network*. Almost like a club membership, a doctor or facility that provides care is either in or out-of-network based on whether or not they have a contract with the insurance company.

HMO health insurance companies (HMOs, discussed in the following chapter) have select doctors and facilities under contract; these are considered in-network.

Doctors and facilities that are in-network have negotiated a contract rate with the insurance company. Basically, these facilities and doctors work for the insurance company at a negotiated cost per patient (the insured).

With urgent care facilities, not every physician or nurse is in-network. Take time to confirm various physicians are in-network before seeing the physician. The insurance company should be able to confirm if a given doctor is in-network.

Another resource for confirming if a physician is in-network is to check www.HealthGrades.com. The website provides a doctor's business address and telephone number, doctor ratings, doctor reviews, the health insurance accepted, hospital residency, and how long the doctor has been in practice.

HealthGrades.com also provides information on hospitals and urgent care facilities. Of course, the best resource is the insurance company. Keep in mind that doctors, hospitals, or physicians do not have to remain in a contract with an insurance company throughout the entire year. They may contract in or contract out at any time; therefore, check

with the insurance company before receiving
care.

Chapter 10 – HMOs, EPOs, and PPOs

"Let's see…red, yellow, and blue; these are primary colors of the color wheel. From these three colors, we can create other colors.

"Red evenly mixed with yellow gives us orange! Okay?

"Blue blended with yellow makes green! Pretty like a leaf, right?

"And let's see…red mingled with blue gives us purple! If you mix all the colors together you get brown! Yeah!

"Oh no, honey…give Mommy the paint brush…we don't want it in your hair!"

Just like primary colors, there are three major health organization types—HMOs (Health Maintenance Organizations), EPOs (Exclusive Provider Organizations), and PPOs (Preferred Provider Organizations).

HMOs have doctors, urgent cares, and hospital facilities that have agreed to offer services within the HMO network. Each doctor and facility lowers their rates for patients in the HMO network. HMOs can also limit how many visits its member can have in a given year. In most cases, a primary care physician (PCP) is selected for the year. If there's a need to see a specialist, the PCP must refer the member to a specialist before the member can setup an appointment. If you (the insured) decide to see a doctor or specialist outside the HMO network, the insured has no insurance coverage and nothing is applied toward the MOOP.

Keep in mind HMO doctors and facilities are paid jointly by the patient and the insurance company through either copays or coinsurance.

An HMO copay (let's say the copay is $30) is jointly paid as a doctor's office visit fee. The doctor's office contracts with the HMO insurance company at an agreed salary. If a doctor has agreed to accept a $175 office payment every time a patient visits their office—the insured pays $30 (copay) and the insurance company pays $145 to meet the $175 fee. The more patients an HMO doctors sees in a day, the more money the doctor makes.

For instance (using the example above), if an HMO doctor sees 20 patients in a day, the doctor receives $2,900 for that day's HMO services provided.

HMO networks are typically restricted to counties (or if a broader network, to states). When purchasing a health insurance plan, ask if in-network coverage includes every county in the state or if it is restricted to certain counties.

For example, if you live in one county and your HMO exists in another, you may be restricted from seeing a doctor or facility where you live. Typically, there is no coverage for out-of-network doctors and facilities. Enough about HMOs. Let's have a look at EPOs.

EPOs (Exclusive Provider Organizations) are inclined to offer a hybrid form of the HMO. The EPO typically offers more flexibility than the HMO. For example, the EPO does not require assigning a PCP to refer insureds to specialist; the insured calls the shots and can see a specialist within the EPO network.

Unfortunately, like the HMOs, if an insured sees a physician or facility out-of-network, the insured will pay the full cost on their own. As with HMOs any payments made outside the network are not applied toward the Maximum Out of Pocket (MOOP).

So, the biggest difference is the member's flexibility in being able to see any doctor or facility within the EPO network without referrals—the decision power is in the insured's hands.

What about the PPO (Preferred Provider Organization)? PPO plans offer more network choices; as a result, out of pocket costs are typically higher.

Like the EPO there is no requirement to assign a specific PCP; you call the shots of which doctors to see in the network. The nice blend with PPOs is that you have access to many in-network physicians and facilities and additional physicians and facilities that are out-of-network (usually at a higher cost). If higher monthly premiums are not a problem, you may want to consider PPOs so you are in control of your plan and have more care provider choices.

If interested in the absolute lowest cost provided, look at ACA (or American Care Act /Obamacare) plans.

Chapter 11 – ACA (or PPACA/Obamacare) and CHIP

School grades are a necessary evil. Grades gauge where you are on a scale from "Failure to Greatness". Without a scale, how would you know how close or how far you are from obtaining your goal (i.e., Greatness)? Scales provide an idea of how many steps are necessary to obtain "Greatness".

Another necessary evil is US healthcare run by the US government with a goal of providing healthcare to every American citizen.

The ACA (Affordable Care Act), also known as PPACA (Patient Protection and Affordable Care Act) and nicknamed "Obamacare", was signed into law March 23, 2010, and enacted in 2014.

Obamacare provides "guaranteed issue" health care. Obamacare prohibits insurance companies from denying coverage to American citizens with pre-existing conditions.

Obamacare provides preventive care screenings, wellness exams, approved contraceptives, elimination of coverage caps, a limit to out of pocket expenses (or MOOP, see Chapter 7), preventive care vaccinations, mammograms, colonoscopies, wellness visits, diabetes screening, HIV screening, and STI screening (most with waived copays or coinsurance).

Competitive insurance plans can be compared and purchased through the Marketplace. The Marketplace can be reached by calling 800.318.2596 or by going to www.HealthCare.gov/get-coverage/ or www.HealthSherpa.com.

For those with limited household income, government subsidies (or government financial aid) may be available to lower monthly premiums. Typically, qualifications are determined by the entire taxable household income.

Check www.Healthcare.gov for more information related to what is covered and what is not covered through ACA compliant health insurance plans.

Keep in mind each state has a CHIP (Children's Health Insurance Program) or KidsCare program. CHIP provides insurance to children in families that may not typically be able to afford insurance. For more information related to CHIP, call 202.903.0101 or see nashp.org, insureKidsNow.gov, or your state's CHIP program.

Chapter 12 – ACA Premium Tax Credit and Cost-Sharing

Never look down on someone who has hit bottom unless you're looking down to extend a hand to help them up! According to an article published a couple of years ago (November 28, 2017) in MarketWatch, nearly all Americans (96%) give to charities. Out of the 96%, Baby Boomers (ages 55 to 73) are more apt to give financially to charities compared to all other generations.

The ACA extends a hand to individuals and families who need help affording healthcare by offering an "Advance Premium Tax Credit" (APTC) financial assistance. APTCs are offered through the on-exchange (explained in another chapter) Marketplace. The

Marketplace can provide discounts through subsidies or cost sharing reduction (CSR). Subsidies lower monthly premiums (or payments). CSRs (sometimes called "extra savings") provide discounts that lower deductibles, copays, and coinsurance. CSRs require purchasing Silver plans through the exchange Marketplace.

A word of caution: if at the end of the year more income is earned than anticipated, the government will demand excess monies be paid back. The APTC may also be taken away.

When accepting an APTC, make sure to attach Form 8962 to the following year's tax return.

For example, let's say a monthly premium is $656 and a subsidy decreases the monthly payment to $156 (a $500 saving) and monthly payments are automatically withdrawn. If the subsidy is taken away (as the result of miscalculating income or if you don't file a tax return), the subsidy or CSR may be taken away without warning. As a result, you may discover $656 automatically withdrawn, leaving your account overdrawn. Typically, the insurance company will not return the excess taken out of your autopay even if the autopay was an error. If autopay is not setup, the insurance company will send a bill showing the $656 due and will give a minimum of 30 days to pay and keep the plan active. Keep in mind, if the plan is cancelled by the insurance company without a special qualifying life event, you may be without insurance for the remainder of the year.

To correct subsidy or CSR errors, call the Marketplace and ask for an appeal (which can take anywhere from a month to several months to resolve).

Chapter 13 – ACA On-Exchange versus Off-Exchange

Do you have any idea where the oldest Chinatown marketplace (outside of Asia) is located?

The oldest Chinatown marketplace in the world (outside of Asia) is Binondo, which is located in Manila, Philippines. Binondo was established in 1594—26 years before the Mayflower landed on Plymouth Rock!

In the United States, San Francisco is home to the oldest Chinatown marketplace in North America. The largest, however, is debatable—San Francisco or Lower Manhattan, New York City. Depends who you ask.

Marketplaces of all types allow excellent central locations to exchange monies for various wares—similar to stock exchanges like the Nasdaq, New York, London, Hong Kong, etc.

Likewise, in the United States, there's an exchange for healthcare plans—also known as The ACA Marketplace (or just plain, "Marketplace").

Purchasing healthcare through the Marketplace is considered purchasing "On-Exchange." Simply put, if purchasing an ACA health plan through the Marketplace, you are purchasing "On the Exchange" (or On-Exchange).

ACA compliant health plans purchased directly from an insurance company (e.g. Blue Cross Blue Shield, Aetna, Cigna, etc.) is considered purchasing "off-exchange."

On-exchange policies can be purchased from www.Healthcare.gov or by calling 800.318.2596. During Open Enrollment (or OE, defined in another chapter) expect long waits to get through the line (upwards to over an hour).

Again, if you prefer not purchasing healthcare through the ACA Marketplace, plans may be purchased directly from an insurance company. As of this writing (2019), there is no mandate (or tax penalty) for not purchasing non-compliant ACA plans.

Chapter 14 – ACA Medals: Bronze-Silver-Gold-Platinum

Adrienne Finch on YouTube recommends organizing your iPhone apps in a number of various ways.

Four favorites is to organize the apps by 1) App color; 2) Most used placed on front page to succeeding pages; 3) Folders by type of app; and 4) Alphabetically (not a fan).

ACA plans are categorized by metallic levels (Bronze, Silver, Gold, and Platinum). The lowest level is Bronze. The only other level below Bronze is the Catastrophic level (available to people under 30 years old). Catastrophic plans cover heart attacks, strokes, or cancer, and typically do not cover routine care.

The catastrophic plan and each metallic level has an assigned percentage value (or actuarial value). The percentage values are divided as follows:

Catastrophic Plans = 60%

Bronze Plans = 60%

Silver Plans = 70%

Gold Plans = 80%

Platinum Plans = 90%

What do the percentages mean? The percentage is equal to the total covered benefit cost a health insurance will pay. For example, if you get injured or ill, the plans would breakdown as follows:

Level	Insurance Pays	You Pay
Catastrophic	60%	40%

Bronze	60%	40%
Silver	70%	30%
Gold	80%	20%
Platinum	90%	10%

The lower the metallic level (Bronze or Catastrophic) the lower the monthly premium but the higher the deductible.

The higher the metallic level (Platinum) the higher the premium and the lower the deductible. Therefore, pay up front (premiums) or pay on the backend (deductibles).

Typically, younger people in good health acquire claims as a result of an injury or accident. Older people usually create claims as a result of deteriorating health (more susceptible to heart disease, chronic illnesses, etc.).

Adults 30 or younger tend to start Catastrophic plans, while older adults typically seek after Silver, Gold, or Platinum plans.

You Wouldn't Hike Without a Compass...

In addition to the metallic level plan premiums and deductibles, keep in mind the average Maximum Out of Pocket:

Around $6,600 for an Individual

Around $13,200 for Families

ACA (or Obamacare) plans are available once a year during Open Enrollment (OE) unless Special Enrollment Periods (SEP) apply (covered in another chapter).

Chapter 15 – ACA Open Enrollment and Special Enrollment Period

Each semester, incoming students must enroll in courses by filling out admissions applications before attending class. Same with health insurance. Before you can purchase a plan, you must enroll by filling out an application during Open Enrollment (OE).

ACA Open Enrollment (OE) starts November 1st through mid-December (unless extended for certain states) each year.

Enrollment is available through HealthCare.gov or by calling 800.318.2596.

After Open Enrollment, ACA compliant health insurance requires a Qualified Life Event (QLE) such as change of jobs, marriage, divorce, or additions to the family (i.e., new births, children adoptions, etc.). Responding to a QLE can take place up to 60 days from the date of the QLE. This 60-day period is called the Special Enrollment Period (SEP).

Children can be enrolled into CHIP (Children's Health Insurance Plan) any time of the year whether they qualify for a SEP or not.

Documentation will be required to allow the purchase of a health plan outside of Open Enrollment.

Chapter 16 – HSA and FSA Accounts

By the time Barcelona Spain's La Sagrada Familia's construction is finished, it will have taken 144 years to complete the project (1882 to 2026). At that time, the construction should be 100% paid off, thanks to funding provided by alms and donations!

Fortunately, HSA (Health Savings Account) and FSA (Flexible Spending Account) plans prevent long funding delays for qualified medical expenses. HSAs and FSAs are also pre-taxed, which helps employees decrease the tax owed to the IRS when taxes are taken from their paychecks.

Both plans allow an employee to determine an account contribution amount. Employers are

NOT obligated to contribute to an employee's account.

Employees and family members on the plan use HSA or FSA funds to pay for qualified medical expenses (i.e., copays, deductibles, approved prescriptions, and certain durable medical equipment, etc.). Check with your insurance company concerning what's covered or check the IRS's Publication 502 (www.irs.gov/pub/irs-pdf/p502.pdf).

A major difference between an HSA and FSA accounts is:

With an HSA, employees are eligible for the account only if they have a high deductible health plan (HDHP)—as of this writing, $1,350 (with a $6,750 maximum out of pocket) for individuals, or $2,700 (with a $13,500 maximum out of pocket) for qualified families.

Also, with an HSA, self-employed individuals can contribute.

An FSA requires that a small business owner establishes the plan allowing employees to contribute. FSA plans are not restricted to high deductible health plans (HDHP). They can be an HDHP or not. Also, *self-employed individuals cannot open an FSA.*

Other differences between an HSA and FSA:

Employers own FSAs and any unused funds belong to the employer. The annual election of funds is available at any time even if the employee hasn't contributed the amount yet.

HSAs are basically bank accounts owned by the employee (even if the employer contributes to the account). Employees only have access to monies that have actually been placed in their HSA account.

Depending on how the employer sets up the HSA or FSA:

You Wouldn't Hike Without a Compass...

FSA funds expire at the end of the plan's year and another is created for the following year.

HSA funds are kept by the employee and can rollover to the following year (based on how the plan was setup).

For more details related to HSA and FSA accounts, check www.irs.gov/publications/p969.

Chapter 17 – Health Share Plans

Missionaries around the world make a difference in hundreds of lives. Most missionaries require support to make their missions possible. Their support is pooled together by contributions from many people who share their same view.

Heath shares consist of a group of like-minded individuals who pool monies together to help cover medical costs. Most health shares are faith-based with qualifying standards for membership. Health shares are not for everyone.

Health shares are not health insurance; as a result, health shares are exempt from ACA individual mandates (or individual shared responsibility provision).

You Wouldn't Hike Without a Compass...

Unlike ACA health insurance plans, health shares typically do not cover wellness checkups, preventive care visits, or pre-existing conditions. Additionally, health share plans cannot be used with HSAs, FSAs, or other reimbursement plans.

Health shares create their own rules on what is covered and what is not. For example, some faith-based health shares do not cover addiction centers. On the flipside, health shares can require members to follow certain nutrition plans and follow regular exercise plans—not request but require.

When considering health share plans, make sure to verify anticipated needs are covered and any requirements designated by the plan.

Some of the most popular health shares are:

1) Christian Healthcare Ministries - ChristianHealthCarePlan.com

2) Liberty HealthShare - LibertyHealthShare.org

3) Medi-Share - MediShare.com

4) Samaritan Ministries Medishare - SamaritanMinistries.org

5) United Refuah HealthShare - UnitedRefuahhs.org

For more health shares that are in alignment with your beliefs, google "health shares" online.

Chapter 18 Telemedicine

Many items that are common today were just a figment of the imagination less than 100 years ago. For example, Dick Tracy (the detective created October 14, 1931), fought crime using his audio watch. Today, calls can be answered or made through the Apple Watch.

George Jetson (aired September 23, 1962) introduced the American public to video conferencing as George conversed with his boss Cosmo Spacely.

Today, many health insurance companies support the use of *telemedicine* using video conferencing.

One of the beauties of telemedicine is that it provides access to certified doctors or nurses using a laptop, iPad, or desktop and can provide medical help 24 hours a day.

The use of telemedicine allows patients to bypass sitting in a doctor's waiting room while being exposed to other patients with more serious and possibly contagious illnesses.

Let's say you've noticed an unusual rash on your arm or an extreme sore throat. Using video conferencing, a doctor or nurse can observe the rash or look at the back of your throat, diagnose the problem, and call in a prescription—no exposure to someone with something serious in a doctor's waiting room or an urgent care room. The telemedicine doctor or nurse can also call in a prescription. Typically, you pay for the prescription and there is usually no copays nor coinsurance fees to be paid.

Even if you don't have access to a PC, laptop, or other video conferencing devices, all you have to do is call a telemedicine doctor or nurse and ask and answer medical questions to get help—right from the comfort of your home or business.

Let's say you're on vacation and out-of-network; telemedicine provides help without the concern of being out-of-network. Thanks, George Jetson!

You Wouldn't Hike Without a Compass...

Keep in mind there are a few states that prohibit telemedicine. Verify telemedicine coverage with your health insurance company.

If the health insurance company does not offer telemedicine coverage, shop around and check pricing. Having telemedicine coverage may save monies in the long run.

Following is a list of telemedicine companies in existence:

CareClix - CareClix.com

TelaDoc - TelADoc.com

MeMD - MeMD.net

iCliniq - icliniq.com (worldwide)

American Well or AmWell - Americanwell.com

MDLive - MDlive.com

DoctorOnDemand - DoctorOnDemand.com (no insurance required)

LiveHealth Online - LiveHealthOnline.com

Virtuwell - VirtuWell.com

D.L. Byrd

PlushCare - PlushCare.com

Health Tap - HealthTap.com

Providence Express Care - Virtual.Providence.org

If your health insurance provides telemedicine, consider contacting telemedicine doctors before PCPs to save monies. The order of contact should be:

1) Telemedicine Physicians or Nurses

2) Primary Care Physicians

3) Urgent Care

4) Hospitals

In emergencies, ignore the above order and call 911.

Chapter 19 – Mom-and-Pop Pretax Health Care Coverage

For those who have fled Corporate America by becoming an entrepreneur and hiring a staff, you can attract promising staff by offering health coverage. How? Through an employer-sponsored benefit plan called the Section 125 Cafeteria Plan.

The Section 125 plan lets employees pay for qualified health insurance plans on a pre-tax basis. Contributions to the cafeteria plan are made before taxes are taken out of their paychecks.

Section 125 also allows employers to contribute money to their employees' health plans to reduce monthly premiums.

D.L. Byrd

For more information concerning Section 125 Plans, contact your payroll service (e.g. ADP) or CPAs who handle your taxes.

Section Two – A Few Things to Understand Your Plan

Section two: terminologies once the policy is in force, or begins.

By now, a lot of terminology has been covered. The following chapters will briefly touch upon terminologies that pop up once the policy begins.

Once open enrollment is completed, the insurance company's customer service lines should have shorter wait times. This may be ideal time to contact the insurance company with questions related to coverage.

One of the first questions should be, "How do I get a HIPAA form?" (defined in another chapter). HIPAA forms are critical to getting claim information.

If supplies such as diabetes monitors (or strips) are needed, ask if there's a preferred monitor brand—preferred monitors are usually supplied at no charge.

Get information related to prescription drugs you're taking (see the chapter on Prescription Management Companies). Not all prescription drugs are covered by certain insurance companies. Even if a former insurance company covered a specific prescription drug, that does not mean a different insurance company will cover the same drug. Ask questions.

Understanding healthcare terms allows you to handle your healthcare and places the power of taking care of you in your hands. You're the boss.

Chapter 20 – Get HIPAA Forms

English Beefeaters (officially known as Yeoman Warders) were Royal Guardians of the Tower of London's Crown Jewels. Yeoman Warders were recognized by their beautiful red and black uniforms with their black tailored flat hats.

Their job was to protect the Crown Jewels and all other royal treasures. As a result, they lived and still live on the Tower of London grounds.

Today, the 37 Yeomen Warders are Ceremonial Greeters at the Tower of London. The Crown Jewels are now protected by technology (i.e. cameras, security glass and lasers, etc.).

Since 1996, all medical information is protected as a result of the Health Insurance Portability and Accountability Act (known as HIPAA). HIPAA requires a release form to share medical information. Many are familiar with HIPAA release forms from visiting doctors' offices. The same is required to release insurance claims information.

As a result, when setting up a health plan, ask the insurance company to provide a HIPAA release form. Even if you're married, insurance companies cannot give claim information to spouses or adult children without this form.

You may ask, "Why would we need a HIPAA form?"

If a family member does not speak English or if a spouse is given the task of checking details on the other spouse's claim, the insurance company cannot (by law) give out information without a HIPAA release form. It's best to request and submit the HIPAA form when the plan begins. Each insurance company has their own HIPAA release form.

An alternative to the HIPAA release form, is verbal confirmation by the person whose information is shared; however, understand that the verbal consent is only good for the duration of the *one* call.

Regarding teenagers, health insurance companies are not allowed to give out information to parents or guardians related to treatment of sexually transmitted diseases, substance-use disorders, or mental illness, without the teen's consent.

For more information, see www.HHS.gov/hipaa/ (the U.S. Department of Health & Human Services) or call 877.696.6775.

Chapter 21 – Negotiated Rates and Balance Billing

Windmill palm trees (a.k.a. trachycarpus fortunei palm trees) are terrible in neighborhoods with Homeowners' Associations (HOA). Why? Twice a year traveling landscaping companies knock on neighborhood doors offering to trim the tree for astronomical costs. To avoid a penalty from the HOA, the homeowner barters and negotiates down the cost of the service. The taller the tree, the higher the costs, and the fiercer the negotiating process.

Health insurance companies negotiate costs for service rendered by doctors, specialists, urgent cares, and hospitals. Unlike office visit costs (which are agreed upon when the doctor or facility contract is approved), the negotiation process for other costs takes place between the submission of a claim (described in another chapter) and when the claim is paid.

For example, if a minor is rushed to a hospital resulting from a hand injury created during a sport and the ER doctor surgically repairs the broken bones, the ER doctor could send in an $8,000 claim. The insurance company in turn will try negotiating the claim down—let's say to $900. If the surgeon agrees to take the negotiated fee the insurance company offered, the insurance company will create an Explanation of Benefit form (discussed in a previous chapter) showing the original cost, the negotiated rate, the amount the policyholder owes to the surgeon, and how much the insurance paid (if the deductible has been met).

If the surgeon is an out-of-network surgeon and the insurance plan does not cover out-of-network charges, the surgeon can reject the amount and insist the policyholder pays the full $8,000. In the event this happens, contact the insurance company to help resolve.

Typically, the insurance company attempts to negotiate down all claims submitted.

When a physician or facility bills you for the difference between the initial charge (e.g.

$8,000 in the previous example) and the negotiated rate (e.g. $900 in the previous example), the difference (e.g. $7,100 using the previous example) is called *balance billing*.

An in-network physician or facility should not balance bill. If this occurs, contact the health insurance company.

As of this writing, President Trump and his staff are working to stop balance billing. Try googling "balance billing" to see if any progress has been made.

Chapter 22 – Claims

Years ago, a neighbor claimed he saw a fish in the local lake that was 5 feet long…FIVE FEET LONG? I wondered for a while if we should change the neighbor's name from Johnny to Noah.

A year later, I discovered the neighbor's claim was slightly off after viewing a picture of another neighbor holding a 4-foot catfish from the same lake. I googled "How big can a catfish get" (https://on.natgeo.com/337Gc3z) and discovered that the largest catfish caught to date was a giant 9-foot catfish weighing in at 646 pounds. I no longer have an interest in swimming in our local lakes.

Unlike the verb, the health insurance term "claim" is a bill doctors, specialists, facilities, etc. submit to insurance companies requesting payment for a service rendered to a policyholder. A claim is just another word for a bill.

Let's paint a scenario. Following a fall, you contact your telemedicine service. After showing the telemedicine physician your wrist and identifying where the pain exists, the telemedicine physician urges you to see a primary care physician. After visiting your primary care physician (PCP) and receiving a hand splint, the PCP's office collects your copay and submits a "claim" (or bill) to your insurance company. The insurance company processes the claim and sends you an Explanation of Benefits (EOB) detailing the service date, doctor, and service provided.

In a nutshell, that's the process of an insurance claim.

Chapter 23 – Prescription Drugs

Popeye the Sailor Man (created January 17, 1929) was a wimpy little guy who hung out with a guy named, J. Wellington Wimpy, simply referenced to as Wimpy—show me your friends and I'll tell you who you are…but anyway…

Popeye was an ordinary guy with an extraordinary secret. When he needed strength to battle against bullies (like Brutus), he would quickly consume a can of "spinach." Popeye was always supplied with an endless number of cans of spinach (maybe through mail order) to improve his strength.

Thanks to modern medicine, there are many prescription drugs that improve daily health.

Each insurance company has a list of drugs covered under their plans—some drugs are covered, others are not. If a prescription drug is not covered ask for an alternative and confirm the replacement with your doctor.

Most insurance companies work with prescription benefit management companies (e.g. CVS Caremark - Caremark.com). Ask for the name and telephone number of the prescription benefit company; these companies are the ones who approve and disapprove prescriptions and can better answer any prescription related questions.

Ask for helpful recommendations from companies such as www.GoodRx.com or www.Drugs.com to help find best drug prices in your area. Sometimes there are coupons or discounts available through the pharmaceutical companies that can lower drug cost. See if the management company has a prescription mailing program; mailing programs also help lower prescription costs of frequently taken drugs.

Keep in mind, prescription drugs are rated in "tiers". The higher the tier (brand drugs without a generic), the higher the price and vice versa.

See if generic drugs are available in the lower tiers. Some insurance companies provide lower-tiered prescriptions at no cost (usually selective generic drugs).

Chapter 24 - Durable Medical Equipment (DME)

No one knows for sure when the first ladder was invented. However, in the Cuevas de la Araña (Araña Caves, or the Spider Caves) of Valencia, Spain, there is rock art called "The Man of Bicorp" that depicts a human figure on a ladder reaching for honey. The rock art painting dates back 8000 years.

Ladders are a necessity to access items beyond our reach.

Durable Medical Equipment (DMEs) are medical equipment used to help insureds have a better quality of life. A DME can be wheelchairs, crutches, nebulizers, oxygen, sleep apnea CPAP machines, diabetic self-testing equipment, and many other items.

You Wouldn't Hike Without a Compass...

Most DMEs are covered under health plans. The best way to obtain a DME is to have a physician write a prescription for the DME. Follow up by contacting your health insurance company to verify coverage and to obtain a list of approved DME companies in your area.

Keep in mind, if it's a medical necessity, it's probably covered under your plan.

Chapter 25 – Elimination Periods

The batter is in the batter's box. All that's needed is one more point to win the game. The crowd is sitting on the edge of their seats. Can this batter hit the winning run?

There's a hush and subtle roar in the stadium. The pitcher throws the ball and the batter smacks the ball high into center field. The batter runs to third base and then back to the home plate.

WHAT? Third to home? You can't eliminate first and second base! There are rules to this game!

You *must* follow the process and run to first base, then to second base, then third, then home! Once legally on the home plate, you can dance the jig if you want. You must follow the rules first. That's how baseball works.

There are always rules to follow and some injuries or illnesses require a wait time called an *Elimination Period* before treatment or payment is provided (e.g. 90 days).

Elimination periods are typically seen in long-term care (LTC) insurance. Elimination periods may come into play when moved from a hospital (after surgery or an illness) to a rehab center.

Typically, the shorter the elimination period, the costlier the plan, and the longer the elimination period, the less expensive the plan.

Elimination periods begin on the day the injury or illness is diagnosed. For more details, contact your insurance company.

Chapter 26 – Insurance Package

Unless you have a driver's license, you can't legally drive the city or town streets.

Without a state certification to sell insurance, you cannot sell insurance in your state.

If you think you can withdraw money from a savings account without proof of ownership, you can forget about attempting access.

Same with insurance policies; without verification that you have a plan, an insurance company will not pay their half of the copay or coinsurance.

When you sign up with a health insurance company, be on the lookout for a package containing your health insurance cards and some type of Certificate of Coverage (sometimes referenced as Summary of Benefits). Both items are very important and should be kept in a safe place for easy access.

Verify the insurance card(s) has the correct information (i.e., correct spelling of name, correct date of birth, insurance policy number, insurance provider numbers, etc.). When visiting a physician, urgent care, or hospital, office personnel will ask to make a copy of your card.

The Certificate of Coverage (or Summary of Benefits) included in your welcome package should provide a list of everything covered in the plan. Although most of the information listed is boring reading, try to read and know what's covered in the plan. Any questions related to coverage should be taken up with the insurance company.

Chapter 27 – Information That Didn't Find a Chapter

Once you have an understanding of health insurance terms, finding the best health insurance to fit your needs can be a huge blessing. Health insurance can be a great tool to prevent extreme financial losses due to unforeseen illnesses or accidents.

This book was created to give leverage when shopping for plans. Knowledge truly is power.

For questions related to coverage or your policy, always contact your health insurance company—it's better to be equipped with correct information than to find yourself stuck with a bill you never anticipated.

There are other health insurance terms that were not covered in this book. Many can be googled (now that you have a good foundation), but, again, utilize the customer service number provided on your insurance card.

In closing, be cautious of hospitals that look like urgent care centers. Brick and mortar hospitals that look like urgent care have been popping up around the country. The difference between urgent care versus hospital visits can be financially astronomical. Even if you feel silly asking, verify care falls under urgent care and not a hospital visit (unless you intended to visit a hospital).

Congratulations on learning health insurance terms! To fully commit terms to memory, consider reading the book two or three times! Again, congratulations!

About the Author

DL is a licensed Health and Life agent in over 20 US states. DL loves traveling and has seen all 50 US States and has traveled to 10 countries.

DL has a passion for helping and educating people to help them have the power of making wise decisions to improve their lives and encouraging those who succeed to play if forward by helping others.

As a result, DL ask that you share the information you learn in this book to help others protect themselves and their family by selecting the right plan without over or under covering their most important asset— themselves and their family.

The intent of this book is to get you started on understanding health coverage terminology. This book gives the basics and does not cover all terms. Additionally, terminology related to Original Medicare and Medicare Advantage is not covered (see Medicare.gov or AARP.com for Medicare terminology).

MIB Search Results

_____

_____

_____

_____

_____

_____

_____

_____

_____

_____

_____

PREMIUM AND COVERAGE QUOTES

Company #1	Talked to
Date / Time	Deductible
	$
Who's Covered	Type of Insurance
What's Covered	
HMO / EPO / PPO	

Company #2	Talked to
Date / Time	Deductible
	$
Who's Covered	Type of Insurance
What's Covered	
HMO / EPO / PPO	

Company #3	Talked to
Date / Time	Deductible
	$
Who's Covered	Type of Insurance
What's Covered	
HMO / EPO / PPO	

John 8:32